D1517186

DATE DUE

A65500 361827

GORILLAS AND CHIMPANZEES

Design
David West
Children's Book Design
Illustrations
Louise Nevett
Tessa Barwick
Picture Research
Cecilia Weston-Baker
Editor
Kate Petty

© Aladdin Books Ltd

Designed and produced by
Aladdin Books Ltd
70 Old Compton Street
London W1

*First published in the
United States in 1987 by*
Gloucester Press
387 Park Avenue South
New York NY 10016

Printed in Belgium

ISBN 0-531-17051-9
Library of Congress Catalog
Card Number 87-80466

This book tells you about our closest primate relatives – gorillas and chimpanzees – how they live and how they are threatened in today's changing world. Find out some surprising facts in the boxes on each page. The Identification Chart at the back shows the differences between gorillas and chimpanzees.

The little square shows you the size of the ape compared with a human.

The picture opposite shows a baby chimpanzee

J
599.8   1. Chimpanzees
CHI   c.   2. Gorilla

88849

FIRST SIGHT

GORILLAS AND CHIMPANZEES

David Chivers

GLOUCESTER PRESS

New York · London · Toronto · Sydney

Introduction

Apes, monkeys and humans all belong to the same order of animals, called primates. Gorillas and chimpanzees belong to the ape family, which also includes orang-utans and gibbons.

Gorillas and chimpanzees are found only in Africa. There is one sort of gorilla and it is found in west Africa, eastern Zaire and the mountains of the Rift Valley. There are two sorts of chimpanzee. The pygmy chimpanzee lives south of the Zaire River. The common chimpanzee is found in the far west, center and eastern part of Africa. Both gorillas and chimpanzees are seriously threatened by the clearance of the tropical forests which are their homes.

◁ **Portrait of a gorilla leader**

Life in the trees

Gorillas and chimpanzees are well suited to life in the trees. They are good at climbing and swinging and hanging. Their very long arms are useful for reaching food at the ends of branches. They can grasp with their feet as well as their hands. Like us, they have thumbs that can be moved against the other fingers. This helps to grasp and pick up things.

Male chimpanzees weigh 90 pounds (40kg) but male gorillas weigh 350 pounds (160kg), twice the weight of an average human. Gorillas are so large that they have to spend a lot of time on the ground. Chimpanzees and gorillas mostly travel by knuckle-walking on all fours with the hands clenched in a fist and the feet curled up.

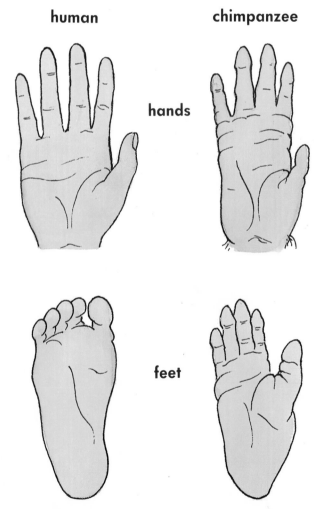

human   **chimpanzee**

hands

feet

Chimpanzees are more at home in the trees than gorillas. They sometimes travel short distances by swinging from branch to branch.

◁ **Young mountain gorillas in Rwanda**

Eating to live

Although they are so big, gorillas eat mainly leaves and stems. They need to spend most of their time eating. One of their favorite foods is wild celery. A gorilla skull shows that the teeth are big and the jaws are very strong for chewing.

Many chimpanzees have a more varied diet. They eat mainly fruit and some leaves, but they are not completely vegetarian like gorillas. They also eat ants, termites and other insects. Some chimpanzees even eat monkeys, young pigs and antelopes. Chimpanzees have smaller teeth than gorillas. The pointed canine teeth are sometimes used for fighting but they are good for opening fruit and shredding stems.

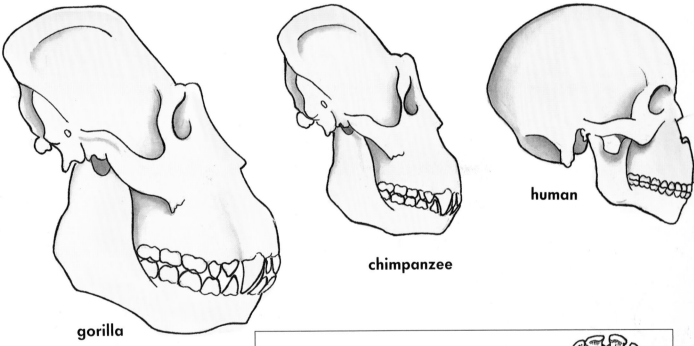

gorilla

chimpanzee

human

Like us, apes can have trouble with their teeth as they get older. Fruit acid damages a chimpanzee's teeth like this. Gorillas' teeth are worn down from chewing coarse stalks.

◁ **Male lowland gorilla eating**

Gathering food

Gorillas in groups look for food together. They eat a little and then they move on. There are always plenty of leaves for them to eat. Some groups find fruit to eat as well.

Chimpanzees look for food separately or in small parties. Most of the time they pick fruit and nuts from trees. (In West Africa they can cause problems when they raid plantations.) They eat blossoms and bark from trees too. Sometimes they peel sticks to "fish" for ants in ant nests or termites in their mounds. They poke the stick into the mound and pull it out covered in the insects. Several chimpanzees will hunt together for monkeys or other animals.

Chimpanzees can't swim. Most of them are afraid of water and avoid it when they can. A few groups are braver and wade into shallow water for food.

"Fishing" for termites with a stick

Chimpanzee carrying fruit ▷

The gorilla group

Gorillas live in well-organized groups. These consist of one adult male, several adult females and their young. There are usually between five and twenty animals altogether. The fur on the adult male turns a silvery white, so he is known as a "silverback." He is the leader of the group and the center of group life. The females gather around him to groom during the midday rest period. He puts on a remarkable display to scare away other males and to attract females to join his group. He beats his chest with his fists, hoots, barks and roars and then tears up vegetation and dashes from side to side. This display has led people to think that gorillas are ferocious. With members of their own group they are very gentle creatures.

Jambo, a male silverback, proved how gentle gorillas can be when a small boy fell into his pit at a British zoo. He sat by the injured boy until he woke up, then moved away for keepers to come to the rescue.

Showing them who's boss – leadership display

| hooting | pretending to feed | throwing sticks |

△ **Mountain gorilla beating his chest**

chest beating   **running sideways**   **ground thumping**   13

Chimpanzee society

Chimpanzees live in groups of up to a hundred animals. The group travels around over an area of 4 to 20 square miles (10-50 sq km). Males often travel together, patrolling the borders of the home range. Sometimes there is fierce fighting between neighboring groups. The females and their young usually search for food separately.

Both male and female chimpanzees are organized so that each animal knows its place. There are several important males in each group, rather than just one leader. Chimpanzees spend many hours grooming one another. This helps to keep them clean but it also strengthens the friendships between them.

hooting – a call to eat

friends hold hands

grooming

The important males in a group of chimpanzees are usually the noisiest and most violent.

◁ **Female chimpanzees grooming each other**

Building a nest

Chimpanzees build nests high up in trees to sleep in at night. First they bend some branches across to make a platform. Then they make a "mattress" out of leaves and mosses. Babies sleep with their mothers. Chimpanzees build a new nest every night. It takes them less than five minutes.

Big gorillas are too heavy to sleep in the trees. They make their nests out of branches and leaves on the ground. A lining of dry dung is probably to keep them warm during the cold nights in the mountains.

Young chimpanzees and gorillas learn how to build nests by watching the older ones. They play at making nests from a very young age.

Gorillas and chimpanzees which have been brought up in cages don't learn how to build nests. If they are taken back to the forest they don't know what to do.

Chimpanzee building a bed in the trees

Growing up

A baby gorilla or chimpanzee is born helpless. It clings to its mother's belly all the time. By the age of six months the baby can ride on its mother's back. When it is two it stops feeding on the mother's milk and learns how to eat like an adult. At four it can travel about on its own, but it will stay close to the mother until it is six years old. By then the mother might have another baby. Babies are only born every five or six years.

Like humans, they take a long time to grow up. There is much to learn, mostly from the mother. She spends time playing with the baby as well as teaching it to look after itself. Other group members, even the adult males, are usually very helpful with the little ones.

Chimpanzees in the wild can live for more than 40 years. In zoos they have lived to be over 50.

Mother chimpanzee playing with her baby

◁ **Baby pygmy chimpanzee clinging on to its mother**

Showing how they feel

Chimpanzees have very expressive faces. Other chimpanzees can see what they are feeling, whether it is excitement, fear, anger – even joy and sadness.

Chimpanzees call to one another in a great variety of grunts and hoots which almost make a sort of language. Smell and touch are also important in relationships between apes.

Scientists working with chimpanzees have come to understand the way apes communicate with each other. Their expressions are not like ours. For example, when a chimpanzee bares its teeth in a "smile," it is showing fear, not happiness.

sad

fearful

As well as grooming each other chimpanzee friends hold hands and hug when they meet.

playful

excited

Chimpanzee sticking out its tongue ▷

Special intelligence

Gorillas and chimpanzees have large brains. They find inventive ways to solve problems. Chimpanzees use rocks and twigs as "tools" to help them eat. They use leaves in all sorts of ways – for soaking up water and mopping up food, and even for dabbing at wounds. Chimpanzees also make weapons from sticks and stones to scare off other animals, such as baboons, if they try to steal their food.

Chimpanzees and gorillas have been studied in homes and zoos. Some have been shown how to paint. Others have been taught to communicate in sign language. The apes have learned to express their own ideas and feelings as well as just copying the signs.

Chimpanzee using a stone as a weapon

Koko, a captive gorilla in the United States, knew enough sign language to tell her keepers that she wanted a kitten for a pet.

◁ **Chimpanzee collecting water**

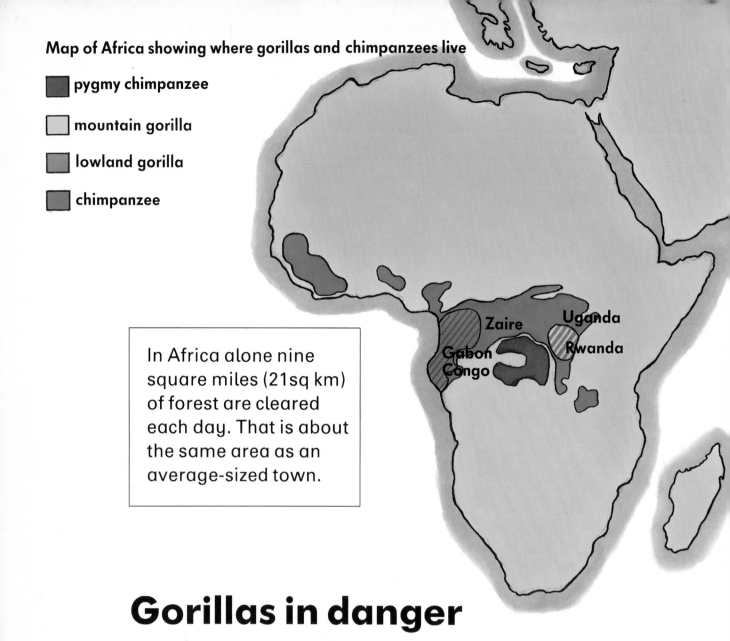

Map of Africa showing where gorillas and chimpanzees live

- pygmy chimpanzee
- mountain gorilla
- lowland gorilla
- chimpanzee

Zaire

Uganda

Gabon

Rwanda

Congo

In Africa alone nine square miles (21sq km) of forest are cleared each day. That is about the same area as an average-sized town.

Gorillas in danger

Because they are so large as well as intelligent, gorillas have little to fear from any other animal. Chimpanzees are sometimes hunted by large cats or hyenas but the gorillas' only enemies are human. Gorillas are chiefly threatened by the destruction of the forests in which they live. They are slow to breed. Any disturbance in their quiet life means that fewer babies survive and the gorilla population gets smaller. There are less than 40,000 gorillas left in the world.

The gorillas which live in the mountains of East Africa are losing their forest homes at an alarming rate. There are probably only 400 of them left. They have retreated higher up the mountains where there is less food for them.

The thick coats of mountain gorillas keep out the cold ▷

Beyond the forest

88849

Some chimpanzees live in more open habitats.
These groups live in wooded grassland
called the savannah. They have to move over much
greater areas to find enough to eat.

These chimpanzees hunt together and kill animals for
their food. They are better at waving sticks and
throwing stones than chimpanzees in forests. In the
savannah they act better as a group to prevent attacks
by lions, cheetahs and hyenas. Savannah chimpanzees
have to stand upright to see over the tall grass.

The development of these chimpanzees has given
scientists more clues about what happened to another
group of primates – humans – when they first moved
out of the forests.

ILLINOIS PRAIRIE DISTRICT LIBRARY

Chimpanzees are more
adaptable than gorillas. Their
numbers are not declining
nearly so rapidly.

**Humans are the only primates
to walk upright all the time**

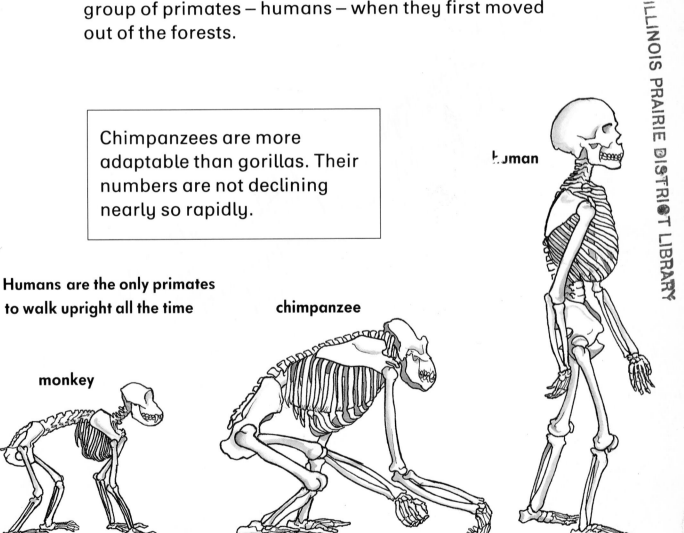

monkey

chimpanzee

human

◁ **Chimpanzee on the savannah**

Survival file

Gorillas and chimpanzees face many dangers. The African forests they live in are disappearing fast. Local people kill them for food and because they are pests. They are protected by law but poachers still kill them and sell their skulls, hands and feet to tourists. They are trapped for zoos and medical research. Some baby chimpanzees are smuggled into the Canary Islands and Spain to be used by beach photographers. The mothers are killed and many of the babies die on the way.

Chimpanzee behind bars

Protecting gorillas and chimpanzees

Scientists study gorillas and chimpanzees in Africa to learn how they live. They want to find out how apes make friends and communicate with each other. They need to know how they move around, how much space they need, what and when they eat.

Some chimpanzees are now protected in National Parks. The scientists working with chimpanzees have helped to set up these reserves. In West Africa they have tried to take captive chimpanzees back to the forests from zoos and pet owners, though this has not been easy.

Studying chimpanzees

Learning about grooming

The governments of Rwanda, Zaire and Uganda have protected the Virunga Volcanoes, almost the last home of the mountain gorilla. They have already set up anti-poaching patrols. They are trying to teach the local people and tourists more about the importance of gorillas. Now other African countries are following these examples, so there is some hope the mountain gorillas will survive.

Identification chart

This chart shows you the differences between the two sorts of chimpanzee and a gorilla. They are drawn to the same scale to show their comparative sizes.

pygmy chimpanzee

chimpanzee

Make a chimpanzee mask

1. Using a pencil and a ruler divide your card into one-inch squares.
2. Copy one of the chimpanzee faces from the opposite page using the squares to help you.
3. Erase the pencil squares from the face.
4. Color in the face.
5. Cut out the mask, make holes and attach strings or elastic.
6. Now you can wear your chimpanzee mask.

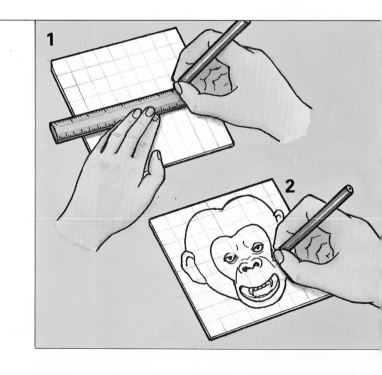

gorilla

angry

excited

playful

alert

3

4

5

6

Index

The picture on the cover shows a female gorilla

Photographic credits: Cover and pages 8, 12, 18, 22 and 31 (bottom): Ardea; title page and pages 6, 10, 14, 16, 20, 24 and 26: Bruce Coleman; contents page: Zefa; page 30: Robert Harding.

PRINTED IN BELGIUM BY proost INTERNATIONAL BOOK PRODUCTION